God Always Keeps His Promises

Cynthia Kirchner/Lasting Legacy Books
1911 SW Campus Dr. #684
Federal Way, WA 98023

Graphic Arts ©2019 Kara McIlroy – karam@foundedonfaith.com

Ordering Information:
Artwork contained in this book can be purchased online at www.lastinglegacybooks. com or by calling 866-466-6206

ISBN: 978-1-946239-28-0

God Always Keeps His Promises

PASTOR MARK SMITH
and the staff of
Faith Baptist Church of Northeast Tacoma, WA

Lasting Legacy Books
Federal Way, WA

Contents

Having therefore these *promises,* dearly beloved, let us cleanse ourselves from all filthiness of the flesh and spirit, perfecting holiness in the fear of God. - 2 Corinthians 7:1

Introduction

I have been young, and now am old; yet have I not seen the righteous forsaken, nor his seed begging bread. - Psalm 37:25

There are two groups of people who will read and enjoy this book. The first group consists of those who can look back over a lifetime of fulfilled promises. They will read this book and rejoice in the blessing of God. The other group consists of those who are hungry to know God and to experience His gracious care for them as dear children.

If our confidence is not in God in this life, then our confidence in His promises in the life to come will falter. When confronted with the harsh realities of life and death our faith will not be sufficient to carry us through.

Let not your heart be troubled: ye believe in God, believe also in me. In my Father's house are many mansions: if it were not so, I would have told you. I go to prepare a place for you. And if I go and prepare a place for you, I will come again, and receive you unto myself; that where I am, there ye may be also. . .Peace I leave with you, my peace I give unto you: not as the world giveth, give I unto you. Let not your heart be troubled, neither let it be afraid. - John 14:1-3, John 14:27

What heartaches are you facing today? What disappointments and failures are discouraging you? How would you life be transformed if you truly believed God would answer every prayer and care for your every need? How differently would you live if you never again had to worry about food, clothing, and shelter? If you were absolutely confident you possessed everlasting life? What if you never experienced apprehension, anxiety, or stress again? Isn't this what God promises in His Word? What keeps us from experiencing the life God has promised to us? **We doubt His promises!** We choose to live by sight and not by faith.

One of our favorite songs is "Because He Lives " written by Bill Gaither. The final verse reads:

> And then one day, I'll cross the river,
> I'll fight life's final war with pain;
> And then, as death gives way to victory,
> I'll see the lights of glory and I'll know He lives!

These few words describe the moment we move from faith to sight: the moment when we see the promise of everlasting life fulfilled, the moment when we move from hope to certainty, the moment when our belief becomes reality. If you have ever hoped for something and then experienced it, you know this feeling: the feeling of a child on Christmas morning who has so hoped for that special gift and found it there waiting for him or her under the tree. Hope became sight.

Our problem is not with God or with His promises. Our problem is with our failure to believe the promises of God.

There are many ways our compassionate Savior strengthens our unbelief. In particular, He has given us His Word.[1]

---

1   *Search the scriptures; for in them ye think ye have eternal life: and they are they which testify of me.* - John 5:39

He has also given to us His indwelling Holy Spirit. *Even the Spirit of truth; whom the world cannot receive, because it seeth him not, neither knoweth him: but ye know him; for he dwelleth with you, and shall be in you.* - John 14:17

The following chapters are meant to help grow and strengthen our faith. They are meant to lead us to a deeper understanding of the riches that are ours in Christ Jesus. They are intended to teach us that . . .

God Always Keeps His Promises!

And the LORD,
he it is that doth
go before thee;
*he will be
with thee,*
he will not fail thee, neither
forsake thee: fear not, neither
be dismayed. - Deut. 31:8

The Basic Premise

Of the many promises God has given to us, the promise of living in His presence for all eternity is undoubtedly the greatest. From this single promise flows all of the other promises of God. Believing His many other promises is the natural result of we believing His wonderful promise of Salvation.

Today, Christians who believe in miracles are often regarded as irrational fanatics or gullible simpletons. Frauds and charlatans are at work all around us. Even our once reliable and unbiased news outlets now produce capricious and biased reports. We must view every account related to us with skepticism. In like manner sophisticated and educated people may view all miraculous events with skepticism.

In many cases the term 'miracle' has been redefined to describe the results of our own efforts. There are miracle weight loss supplements, miracle drugs, miracle skin-care products, and miracle foods, to name just a few. Even though the results from these may be remarkable, they are not miraculous. Merriam-Webster defines a miracle as an extraordinary event manifesting divine intervention in human affairs. In other words, a miracle is something that only God can perform.

There are those who believe that the age of miracles belonged to the early church. They assign events such as Daniel surviving the lions' den, Moses parting the red sea, and Jesus' resurrection as belonging to a different dispensation and not to be expected in this present day. They explain away the promises found in God's Word as not pertaining to the modern church.

To be sure, many false teachings concerning modern miracles permeate today's church just as they did in the first century. The Internet has given rise to myriads of fantastic tales based on nothing more than the imagination of the storyteller. Paul's admonition to the church at Ephesus applies to us today just as much as it did in Ephesus. *That we henceforth be no more children, tossed to and fro, and carried about with every wind of doctrine, by the sleight of men, and cunning craftiness, whereby they lie in wait to deceive;* - Ephesians 4:14

Christianity without miracles is not Christianity. These falsehoods, however, do not in any way disprove the existence of the miraculous in our world today. Quite frankly, Christianity without miracles is not Christianity. It is a form of godliness without any power to back it up.[2]

THE FULLNESS OF THE CHRISTIAN LIFE IS FOUND IN BELIEVING

There is so much more to the Christian life than attending church on Sunday. Jesus assured us, *I am come that they might have life, and that they might have it more abundantly.* - John 10:10. How many people have achieved their life goals in their own strength only to ask themselves, "Is this all there is?" God has promised us so much more! God has made available to us so much more!

God reveals Himself to an unbelieving world by keeping His promises. Over and over in the Bible, miracles were the evidence God gave to confirm that He is the Lord God.

2   *Having a form of godliness, but denying the power thereof: from such turn away.* - Timothy 3:5

Recall Elijah's contest with the prophets of Baal, when God sent His fire from Heaven to consume Elijah's sacrifice - *And when all the people saw it, they fell on their faces: and they said, The LORD, he is the God; the LORD, he is the God.* - 1 Kings 18:39.

God reveals Himself to an unbelieving world by keeping His promises.

Or consider Nebuchadnezzar's reaction when God delivered Shadrach, Meshach, and Abednego from the fiery furnace - *Then Nebuchadnezzar spake, and said, Blessed be the God of Shadrach, Meshach, and Abednego . . . because there is no other God that can deliver after this sort.* - Daniel 3:28-29

The miraculous is and always has been the evidence of genuine faith. When the doubters and scoffers questioned Jesus' authority to forgive sins, His response was to miraculously heal the man sick of the palsy.[3]

The very basis of the Christian faith is the miracle of the resurrection. Either Christ arose as He promised or Christianity is a fable. As Paul told the Corinthians - *And if Christ be not risen, then is our preaching vain, and your faith is also vain.* - 1 Corinthians 15:14

The most adventurous, the most resilient, the most exciting, and the most fulfilling Christian life is lived by those who are willing to step out by faith and take God at His Word. These are the missionaries. These are the prayer warriors. These are the church planters. These are the Bible translators and printers. These are the founders of orphanages, Christian schools, hospitals, and colleges. They live life abundantly, experiencing the joy of serving and bringing forth fruit as God intends. They attempt the impossible, believing in the God of the impossible and His promises.

> Carmen was a young wife learning to live by faith. She was concerned because her husband was sometimes reckless when driving. He often drove well over the speed limit, dashed in and out of traffic, and tailgated the car in front of him. At first Carmen tried to correct his bad driving habits. As any married woman will testify, husbands do not appreciate their wife telling them how to drive. Instead she began praying privately for her husband. He knew something had changed because she stopped.

---

3   But that ye may know that the Son of man hath power on earth to forgive sins, (then saith he to the sick of the palsy,) Arise, take up thy bed, and go unto thine house. - Matthew 9:6

He knew something had changed because she stopped mentioning his driving. He suspected she was praying.

One night he came home from work and confronted her. "Have you been praying for my driving?" She told him truthfully that she had. "That's what I thought! I just got a speeding ticket!" Her husband was wise enough to understand God answered prayer, especially the prayer of a loving wife. He often pointed out blessings that came their way, asking her, "Did you pray for this or that?" He was not surprised when she honestly answered, "Yes." He called her many answers to prayer "The Carmen Policy" meaning their family was experiencing God's favor because Carmen trusted in God's promises.

Psalm 1 describes this manner of living. *Blessed is the man that walketh not in the counsel of the ungodly, nor standeth in the way of sinners, nor sitteth in the seat of the scornful. But his delight is in the law of the LORD; and in his law doth he meditate day and night. And he shall be like a tree planted by the rivers of water, that bringeth forth his fruit in his season; his leaf also shall not wither; and whatsoever he doeth shall prosper.* - Psalm 1:1-3

This is the life God intends for His children.

BELIEVING IS A CHOICE

We rarely consider the things we are robbed of because of doubt. Doubt is often regarded as a positive trait; it is deemed a reasonable response to the promises of God. And no wonder, when we reflect upon the many promises made by men and never fulfilled. *But God is not a man, that He should lie!* - Numbers 23:19. It is God's very nature to keep His promises and God has not changed. The Word of God clearly states that God is faithful and will keep His promises through all generations.[4] God's character is not different today. Miracles are just as possible today as they ever have been. What limits God's working in our lives is our own unbelief.

Miracles are just as possible today as they have ever been!

---

4   *Know therefore that the LORD thy God, he is God, the faithful God, which keepeth covenant and mercy with them that love him and keep his commandments to a thousand generations;* - *Deuteronomy 7:9.*

Just as belief is a choice, so are doubt and unbelief. We may choose unbelief even when the logical choice would be to believe. In the Bible we read the account of Jesus' own countrymen choosing unbelief despite the many visible proofs they witnessed.

And when he was come into his own country, he taught them in their synagogue, insomuch that they were astonished, and said, Whence hath this man this wisdom, and these mighty works? Is not this the carpenter's son? is not his mother called Mary? and his brethren, James, and Joses, and Simon, and Judas? And his sisters, are they not all with us? Whence then hath this man all these things? And they were offended in him. But Jesus said unto them, A prophet is not without honour, save in his own country, and in his own house. And he did not many mighty works there because of their unbelief. - Matthew 13:54-58

The power of God was manifest over and over in Christ's ministry and it was available to those living in His "own country" (vs. 54) but because of unbelief they did not "see" a manifestation of God's power. James said it this way, *yet ye have not, because ye ask not.* - James 4:2

Think of those who discovered the awesome, amazing power of God, simply by believing. Consider the woman with the issue of blood, *And a certain woman, which had an issue of blood twelve years, And had suffered many things of many physicians, and had spent all that she had, and was nothing bettered, but rather grew worse, When she had heard of Jesus, came in the press behind, and touched his garment. For she said, If I may touch but his clothes, I shall be whole. And straightway the fountain of her blood was dried up; and she felt in her body that she was healed of that plague.* - Mark 5:25-29

And recall Jairus' daughter. *While he yet spake, there came from the ruler of the synagogue's house certain which said, Thy daughter is dead: why troublest thou the Master any further? As soon as Jesus heard the word that was spoken, he saith unto the ruler of the synagogue, Be not afraid, only believe. . . And he took the damsel by the hand, and said unto her, Talitha cumi; which is, being interpreted, Damsel, I say unto thee, arise. And straightway the damsel arose, and walked; for she was of the age of twelve years. And they were astonished with a great astonishment.* - Mark 5:35-36, 41-42. In verse 36 the instruction is simple, *"only believe"* and in verse 42 we discover their response. ***"And they were astonished with a great astonishment."***

5

These people believed because of what they had seen. Even Thomas believed once

Jesus' manifestation, miracles and ministry were all meant to help them believe!

he had seen the power of God manifest in the Son of God, *And Thomas answered and said unto him, My Lord and my God.* - John 20:28. And still, some would not believe, even what they had seen with their own eyes. *Having eyes, see ye not? and having ears, hear ye not?* - Mark 8:18. Jesus' manifestation, miracles, and ministry were all meant to help them believe! For some seeing is believing, and for others seeing is not enough for believing.

Believing Opens to Us Eternal Life

The miracle of "new life in Christ" can only come by believing.[5] In John 1:7 we read that John the Baptist came to make Jesus known. He was manifest as a light to point all men to THE LIGHT, but they had to believe. The miracles of Christ would follow the ministry of John, and many would believe. Yet Jesus said to the multitude that they didn't even believe what they had seen.[6] How could they believe what they would not receive?

Scripture confirms that the prerequisite of receiving is believing! All eternity hangs in the balance.[7] Jesus challenged Nicodemus to believe. *If I have told you earthly things, and ye believe not, how shall ye believe, if I tell you of heavenly things?* - John 3:12. This exchange was in preparation for one of the greatest of God's promises found in John 3:16 *...whosoever believeth in him should not perish, but have everlasting life.*

Belief Opens Us to the Impossible

---

5   *I said therefore unto you, that ye shall die in your sins: for if ye believe not that I am he, ye shall die in your sins.* - John 8:24.

6   *And ye have not his word abiding in you: for whom he hath sent, him ye believe not... For had ye believed Moses, ye would have believed me: for he wrote of me. But if ye believe not his writings, how shall ye believe my words? John 5:38, 46-47*

7   *But as many as received him, to them gave he power to become the sons of God, even to them that believe on his name: John 1:12*

The world saw the Man. They saw the ministry. They even saw the miracles, and yet in unbelief they could not truly see the might of His miracles or the majesty of His manifest presence, Immanuel, God with us. What men miss because they will not believe![8]

The world saw the Man. They saw the ministry. They even saw the miracles,

Believing is seeing! Through faith, multitudes saw the mighty power of God manifest through the Messiah - the sent one - the Lord Jesus Christ. There were so many marvelous, miraculous events in our Lord's ministry all meant to reveal to the "believer" the power of God manifest to those who "believe and receive." The multitudes saw miracle after miracle in the ministry of our Lord Jesus Christ, yet many would not believe! To those who saw and believed God was manifest - made known to them.[9]

It was a challenging life for Miranda. Her husband walked out on her and their three school age children. Miranda had never worked outside their home. She did not know how she could earn enough to care for the four of them but, she prayed and sought God believing that a door would open. Even at her most impoverished, Miranda always tithed faithfully. She believed it was her job to obey and God's job to take care of her family. She often quoted, I have been young, and now am old; yet have I not seen the righteous forsaken, nor his seed begging bread. - Psalm 37:25.

A few days later, a friend told Miranda that her boss was looking for a new assistant. Miranda was interviewed and hired that same day. It wasn't long until Miranda was promoted and received a generous raise. She gave more and continued to trust God. Soon an opportunity to rent a nicer home in a safer neighborhood came her way. Then another raise and another. After a few years Miranda was making well over $200,000 a year and giving more than she ever imagined possible. Miranda was eventually giving over $80,000 a year. She believed God for the impossible. She remained faithful and trusted in His promises. God did not fail her.

We may believe all of the miracles recorded in the Word of God and not believe the possibilities open to believers today. What impossible things could we see in our lives today if we were only willing to believe God?

---

8   *Then he said unto them, O fools, and slow of heart to believe all that the prophets have spoken: - Luke 24:25*

9   *But these are written, that ye might believe that Jesus is the Christ, the Son of God; and that believing ye might have life through his name. John 20:31*

Believing the impossible is foolishness when we base our faith on the abilities of men, but believing the impossible is incredibly sensible when we base our faith on God's promises.[10]

What astounding gifts does God have for us if we will believe His promises?

In Lewis Carroll's book <u>Alice in Wonderland</u>, you may recall this exchange between Alice and the Queen.

Alice laughed: "There's no use trying," she said; "one can't believe impossible things."

"I daresay you haven't had much practice," said the Queen. "When I was younger, I always did it for half an hour a day. Why, sometimes I've believed as many as six impossible things before breakfast." *Lewis Carroll, Alice in Wonderland.*

All of us need more practice believing God for the impossible. Ask yourself, "What am I missing because of unbelief? In what area of my life do I need a miracle?"

A Promise Journal

Begin your journey of believing and achieving the impossible by keeping a 'Promise Journal.' As you study the Bible, record the promises the Holy Spirit reveals to you. Many times, as you read His Word, a specific verse will stand out. You may have read the verse many times before but suddenly it now becomes personal. These are precious promises! Record them in a journal and hide them in your heart. If you will believe and receive you will see the fulfillment of His promises.

---

10 *But Jesus beheld them, and said unto them, With men this is impossible; but with God all things are possible. - Matthew 19:26*

Remind Me Dear Lord

The things that I love
And hold dear to my heart
Are just borrowed
They're not mine at all
Jesus only let me use them
To brighten my life
So remind me, remind me dear Lord

Roll back the curtain of memory now and then
Show me where you brought me from and
Where I could have been
Just remember I'm a human and humans forget
So remind me, remind me dear Lord

Nothing good have I done
To deserve God's own Son
I'm not worthy of the scars
In His hands
Yet He chose the road to Calvary
To die in my stead
Why He loved me I can't understand

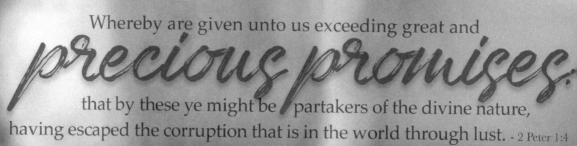

Whereby are given unto us exceeding great and *precious promises,* that by these ye might be partakers of the divine nature, having escaped the corruption that is in the world through lust. - 2 Peter 1:4

The Precious Promises

GOD'S PROMISES ARE FOUNDED ON FAITH

For therein is the righteousness of God revealed from faith to faith: as it is written, The just shall live by faith. - Romans 1:17

For as the body without the spirit is dead, so faith without works is dead also. - James 2:26

The Christian life is lived by faith - faith in the promises of God.

We must not simply base our faith upon what others have told us. Certainly, others' experiences can be encouraging. All of us have seen the before and after photos testifying of the benefits found in the latest 'miracle' cosmetic, but God has given to us much more on which to base our faith. He has given to us His own Word.[11]

---

11 *We have also a more sure word of prophecy; whereunto ye do well that ye take heed, as unto a light that shineth in a dark place, . . . - 2 Peter 1:19*

We should have just as much assurance in the promise of answered prayer today as did Elijah, Daniel, Moses, or the Apostle Paul. Our prayers, however, must be based upon the solid authority of the Word of God and not upon our own suppositions.

Recently, a woman was overheard ranting about the President of United States. Her listener finally stopped her and asked, "On what do you base your opinion? Where do you get your facts?" She could not answer. Her opinions were based upon rumors, gossip, and the opinions of others and not upon any solid facts. We should ask ourselves the same question regarding our own beliefs. Do we base our expectations for answers to our prayers on doubt and fears or do we base our expectations on the Word of God? One day we will see Him as He is, but until that day, He has given to us His written Word as the basis for our faith.[12]

As any advertising executive will tell you, the majority of people are not moved by fact or faith, but rather by feelings. The most successful advertising appeals to our feelings - our emotions. In some cases, we do not even know we want a particular product until we see the advertisements for it! We are moved to feel that if we drive a certain car, our families will be happy and safe; if men will use a particular shampoo, they will become irresistible to women, if we brush our teeth with a certain toothpaste, our white teeth will sparkle, and we will be invited to the most exciting parties. And even though we all <u>know</u> these implied promises are at best exaggerated, and in most cases totally bogus, they continue to appeal to us.

God's promises are different because God always keeps His promises. God knows our genuine needs before we know and acknowledge them ourselves.

By exercising faith in His promises our needs are met.

By exercising faith in His promises our needs are met. Jesus said to the blind men seeking to be healed, *According to your faith be it unto you.* - Matthew 9:29 And later He taught His disciples, *And all things, whatsoever ye shall ask in prayer, believing, ye shall receive.* - Matthew 21:22

GOD'S PROMISES ARE ESSENTIAL IN THE CHRISTIAN LIFE

---

12   *Beloved, now are we the sons of God, and it doth not yet appear what we shall be: but we know that, when he shall appear, we shall be like him; for we shall see him as he is. - 1 John 3:2.*

It is by His promises that we become partakers of His divine nature and it is by His promises that He moves us forward and reveals His plans for us. We see this demonstrated over and over again in our Bible. Consider Abraham. He left his home

It is by His promises that He moves us forward and reveals His plans for us.

and obeyed God because he looked forward to the fulfillment of God's promises.[13] It was because Abraham believed God's promises that he left his home and journeyed toward Canaan.[14]

As we believe God's promises, we also move forward in our Christian walk. When we doubt God, we falter and rather than moving ahead, we wander just as the children of Israel wandered when they questioned God's will and doubted His promises to them. Ten of the men they sent to investigate the land returned with what the Bible calls "an evil report." Two of the men, Caleb and Joshua, returned believing God and encouraging the people to trust God to fulfill His great promises to them. The children of Israel chose to reject God's promises and to believe the men's evil report. [15] As a result, they wandered another 40 years and never entered the land promised to them.

The description of the giants in the land was enough to fill the hearts of the children of Israel with doubt and fear. While they trusted and believed God, they moved forward, but when unbelief overcame their faith, they wanted to go backward. When we focus on God's Word and His promises we live life expectantly. We look

When we focus on God's Word and His promises we live life expectantly.

forward to the wonders and blessings God has in store for us. But when fear and doubt take root in our thinking, we focus on our own pleasures and desires. We

---

13   *By faith he sojourned in the land of promise, as in a strange country, dwelling in tabernacles with Isaac and Jacob, the heirs with him of the same promise: For he looked for a city which hath foundations, whose builder and maker is God.*
- Hebrews 11:9-10

14   *And he brought him forth abroad, and said, Look now toward heaven, and tell the stars, if thou be able to number them: and he said unto him, So shall thy seed be. And he believed in the LORD; and he counted it to him for righteousness. And he said unto him, I am the LORD that brought thee out of Ur of the Chaldees, to give thee this land to inherit it. - Genesis 15:5-7*

15   *And wherefore hath the LORD brought us unto this land, to fall by the sword, that our wives and our children should be a prey? were it not better for us to return into Egypt? And they said one to another, Let us make a captain, and let us return into Egypt. - Numbers 14:3-4*

become disappointed, disillusioned, and discouraged. We reject God's will and focus on our own will.

The children of Israel doubted because God's will was not what they expected. They imagined that life would be easy. They saw the evidence of the good things God provided for them. They saw the incredible fruit brought back by the men who searched the land. [16]

God's promise of a land flowing with milk and honey was tangible, but it also included

Lee, now in her late seventies, had lived a life of faith, but little did she know the greatest test of her faith lay just ahead. She had seen many, many answers to prayer. She had seen her children come to Christ, her family and friends healed of various conditions, and God's provision for the many missionaries she corresponded with monthly. The day the doctor told her she had stage 4 lung cancer and that it had spread to other parts of her body, she knew it was her turn to trust Him. Her family wept. Her many friends wept. But Lee continued to smile and to trust God.

Lee told the Lord it was up to Him to heal her or to take her to Heaven, but that she believed if it was His will He could, without a doubt, heal her completely. She left the outcome to Him and continued to tell everyone who would listen how good and great her God was.

God did not have to heal Lee to be glorified because Lee glorified Him every day regardless. Every doctor, every nurse, and every visitor heard about God and His goodness to Lee. Had God not intervened, Lee's diagnosis would have certainly been a death sentence. The improvements were small at first, but it was obvious the cancer was shrinking. With each check-up the doctors were more and more amazed at how rapidly Lee was recovering. At the time of this writing, it has been just over a year since Lee's diagnosis and the doctors have declared her cancer free!

God is certainly glorified in her miraculous recovery, but He is even more glorified by a woman whose faith could not be shaken! It is often said, "A faith that cannot be tested, cannot be trusted." Lee has a faith that can be trusted!

battles and giants. Without faith we are discouraged by the battles of life. What we may forget is that in or out of the will of God we will face battles and giants. The difference

---

16   *And they told him, and said, We came unto the land whither thou sentest us, and surely it floweth with milk and honey; and this is the fruit of it. - Numbers 13:27*

is that within the will of God we face them with God on our side, but outside of the will of God we face them alone.

God's Promises Apply to All Who Believe

We may think that God's promises do not apply to us because we do not '**deserve**' them. We may feel God will not help us because we brought our problems upon ourselves. This was certainly the case for Adam and Eve. God warned them not to eat of the fruit. They had plenty of delicious things to eat. They enjoyed the peace and beauty of a perfect environment in the garden. They experienced the presence of God and communed with Him on a daily basis. Yet, they were not satisfied. They were definitely deceived into believing that what Satan offered was better than what God had given to them.

We do the same thing today. We attempt to gratify our desires with pleasures we believe to be better than the genuine joys God has promised to us. We learn from the Proverbs that, *"There is a way that seemeth right unto a man, but the end thereof are the ways of death."* - Proverbs 16:25. Adam and Eve thought they had discovered a better way, but it was the wrong way with a bitter end.[17]

The first promise recorded in the Bible is found in Genesis 3:15. Having disobeyed God and eaten of the forbidden fruit, all seemed hopeless for Adam and his wife, Eve. In the midst of God's pronounced judgment against the serpent is found this somewhat mysterious promise of future redemption. *And I will put enmity between thee and the woman, and between thy seed and her seed; it shall bruise thy head, and thou shalt bruise his heel.* - Genesis 3:15

From our vantage point, looking back through the ages, we understand the unfolding truth as this promise is fulfilled in Jesus Christ. At the time, Eve must have clung to the promise that one day her seed would defeat the enemy, for after Cain kills Abel Eve states concerning Seth, *For God hath appointed me another seed instead of Abel, whom Cain slew.* - Genesis 4:25. She believed God and hoped in His promise to them.

---

17   *Enter ye in at the strait gate: for wide is the gate, and broad is the way, that leadeth to destruction, and many there be which go in thereat: - Matthew 7:13*

There's no doubt that it was their choice to disobey God. They deserved the results, just as we deserve the results of our sin and disobedience. God did not leave them hopeless and He does not leave us hopeless. God gave them a promise.

What hope do we have when we have already chosen the wrong way? Our hope is found in the **exceeding great and precious promises:** of God. It is by these that we may become **partakers of the divine nature and escape the corruption that is in the world through lust.** 2 Peter 1:4

WE MUST HIDE HIS PROMISES IN OUR HEARTS

I will delight myself in thy statutes: I will not forget thy word. - Psalm 119:16

To **believe** the promises of God, we must **know** the promises of God. God's promises are found in His Word. When we ignore the Word of God, we weaken our faith and fall prey to the lies of the world. This is one reason I encourage Christians to keep a promise journal. As we read through the Bible on a daily basis, promises will jump out at us. Recording these promises helps us to remember them and to trust God for them. These **exceeding great and precious promises** are treasures to be preserved and protected. Writing them on paper helps us to write them in our hearts.

To believe the promises of God, we must know the promises of God...

Karen and her family attended church faithfully. She believed the Bible and trusted Jesus Christ as her personal Savior. She helped in nursery and Sunday school, and she had many friends at her church. But none of them knew Karen struggled with anxiety and depression. She always smiled, and she was always ready to listen to others who were hurting and in need, but at night Karen experienced nightmares and insomnia. As a young girl, Karen had been molested. It was a violent attack. Like many parents in those days, Karen's parents swept the incident under the rug and the situation was never really resolved. Karen married a wonderful, gentle Christian man and they had two remarkable children. But the fear and terror never completely left Karen. Many years later, she still bore the emotional scars from that attack.

One day, Karen, following the advice of her pastor, sought out an older Christian woman in her church. She opened up her heart and poured out the dark burden she carried all those years. This woman, who had suffered a similar incident, was able to share some of God's precious promises - promises that helped to free her of fear and depression.

Together the two women prayed and claimed these promises in Karen's life. From time to time they would talk again and read these and other promises. Karen claimed the victory that was hers in Jesus Christ. She learned to conquer fear and anxiety believing that nothing could ever separate her from the love of Christ. This is not to say that professional help is not needed in similar circumstances, but there is genuine healing and power in the Word of God and His promises.

The more familiar we are with the Word of God, the more we have to draw upon in times of trouble. Keeping a promise journal allows us to remember and quickly reference the promises God has given to us. There are reference books that list some of the promises of God by topic. These are helpful, but creating our own personal record of precious promises is even more useful.

JOURNALING TIPS

At the front of your journal, you may wish to make a color-coded list of your own topics and needs. For instance, 'Financial Promises' may be colored green, 'Wisdom/Guidance Promises' may be colored purple, and 'Salvation and Protection Promises' may be colored red. Then as you come across a promise that speaks to your heart, record it in your journal and color code it either with a colored underline or a colored symbol. In this way you can flip through your journal and find those promises at a glance.

If you are using symbols you may also mark the corresponding verses in your Bible with the appropriate color and symbol.

$$ Financial Promises
?? Wisdom & Guidance Promises
++ Salvation and Protection Promises
!! Hope and Healing Promises

Being **born again**, not of corruptible seed, but of incorruptible, by the word of God, which liveth and abideth for ever. - 1 Peter 1:23

The Certainty of God's Promises

God's Word is the authority on which His promises are based. If the Word of God is inerrant and infallible, then the promises contained within Its pages can be trusted without reservation. They are absolutely trustworthy.

From the beginning Satan's ploy has been to attack the reliability of God's Word to man. From the day he first whispered to Eve, *"Yea, hath God said?"* - Genesis 3:1, to modern day scoffers and critics, his tactics have not changed. The promises of God cannot be relied upon if the Word of God is not undeniably reliable.

God chose each and every word for a purpose. Even the smallest punctuation mark had a divine origin and purpose.[18]

---

18   *For verily I say unto you, Till heaven and earth pass, one jot or one tittle shall in no wise pass from the law, till all be fulfilled. - Matthew 5:18*

Sometimes the contracts drawn up by attorneys can seem interminably wordy. Anyone who has ever tried to challenge one of those contracts, can tell you that every word is there for a purpose. Contracts are carefully crafted. Phrases like "indemnify" and "hold harmless", while rarely used in everyday speech, are meant to make the terms and conditions of the contract clear and understandable. Why would we assume that God would be any less exact with His eternal Word?

The right word for the right purpose is extremely important and valuable. We find many statements concerning the value of words in the Bible.[19] Words paint pictures on the canvas of our minds. Two words may have similar meanings and yet one will communicate our thoughts much better than the other. For instance, if we read, "Bobby ran away." We might picture a boy running away in fear or anger. But if instead we read "Bobby scampered off", we might picture a boy happily trotting on his way.

Words, like colors, have many shades of meaning. If John dropped the vase, we assume it was an accident. But, if John smashed the vase, we assume it was on purpose and maybe in anger. We may be accurately reporting the event, but our choice of words communicates the meaning behind our words.

Since every word was particularly chosen by God, our study of the Bible must entail asking ourselves, "what meaning does God specifically intend?" Consider the little word 'so' in John 3:16: *For God **so** loved the world, that he gave his only begotten Son, that whosoever believeth in him should not perish, but have everlasting life.* What if we reworded the verse to read, "For God loved the world so much that . . ." much of the intended meaning would be lost. "So much" implies a finite amount of love, while *"God so loved"* denotes infinite or unlimited love. The love of God cannot be quantified. The amount of love God revealed in giving His only begotten Son is not so much. It is so total, so infinite, so beyond human comprehension. It is **SO**.

God does not need an editor. Every word is significant, and every word has been chosen by God for a purpose.

God does not need an editor. Every word is significant, and every word has been chosen by God for a purpose. When we change or rearrange the words to suit our preconceived ideas, we lose the deepest level of meaning. God's Word is not haphazard. God spoke deliberately and on purpose.

---

19   *A word fitly spoken is like apples of gold in pictures of silver. Proverbs 25:11 and Therefore I love thy commandments above gold; yea, above fine gold. Psalm 119:127*

God chose the Words. When man changes the words, he changes the meaning. The purpose, power, and potential of God's Word is diluted and polluted when man swaps out the words God carefully chose.[20]

To claim the promises of God, we must believe the Word of God. If we change the words, we no longer have the Word of God on which to base our belief.

GOD'S WORDS ARE POWERFUL

Words are very powerful. They impact our emotions, our thinking, our beliefs, and even our actions. An eloquent orator can stir the hearts of men to repent and turn to God while in contrast a fanatical propagandist, with their carefully chosen words, can stir a crowd into a violent mob.

As potent as men's words can be, God's Word is infinitely more powerful. By the power of His Word, God created all things. Some artists have portrayed God's hands forming creation. This is in error. The work of creation was by the power of His Word. *By the word of the LORD were the heavens made; and all the host of them by the breath of his mouth.* - Psalm 33:6

God's Word is compared to a two-edged sword in the book of Hebrews. *For the word of God is quick, and powerful, and sharper than any twoedged sword, piercing even to the dividing asunder of soul and spirit, and of the joints and marrow, and is a discerner of the thoughts and intents of the heart.* Hebrews 4:12

God uses His Word to reach into our hearts where nothing else can reach.

God uses His Word to reach into our hearts where nothing else can reach. He uses His Word to bind up broken hearts, to give hope to those who are held captive by sin and addiction, and to set those imprisoned by doubt and ignorance free.[21]

---

20   *The words of the LORD are pure words: as silver tried in a furnace of earth, purified seven times.* - Psalm 12:6

21   *The Spirit of the Lord GOD is upon me; because the LORD hath anointed me to preach good tidings unto the meek; he hath sent me to bind up the brokenhearted, to proclaim liberty to the captives, and the opening of the prison to them that are bound;* - Isaiah 61:1

Preaching the Word of God brings with it the power of God. It is through the spoken Word that souls are saved and lives are changed.[22]

There is power in the spoken Word. When we read silently, the words enter into our minds and hearts through the eye-gate, but when we read out loud, those words enter into our hearts and minds both through both the eye and the ear gates. Jesus said, *He that hath ears to hear, let him hear.* - Matthew 11:15

Read the Bible out loud, pray the Bible out loud, and praise the Lord out loud!

GOD'S WORD BRINGS FAITH AND COMFORT TO THE SOUL OF MAN

By the power of His Word God speaks to our troubled souls. How many times has God laid on your own heart a particular verse? Perhaps it was a verse you'd read many times before, but at your particular point of need, the verse seemed to jump from the page. The promises in these verses are yours to claim and trust. The Lord intended them for you! They are the precious promises. Record them in your journal. Memorize them in your heart. Reread them often.

We find the faith we need to trust God's promises in His Word. God's Word calms the waves and stills the storms. Mark 4:39 God's Word calls those things that are not as they were. Romans 4:17 God's Word heals the wounded and binds up the broken hearted. Isaiah 61:1 We find within Its pages help for our every need.

There are many beloved passages of Scripture that people of faith read and reread. Passages have been memorized and hidden in the hearts of men and women, boys and girls for generations. Among these precious passages are particularly the promises trusted from generation to generation. It is often in the midst of adversity when we seek God's promises. These are the times we look to God for reassurance, comfort, and direction. God's Word is our source of the promises of God.[23]

These things already belong to the believer. Why do we lack what we so desperately need? Because the promises of God in the Word of God are unclaimed. God gave them to us in His Son. When we fail to receive the Word of God, we fail to receive what

---

22   *For the preaching of the cross is to them that perish foolishness; but unto us which are saved it is the power of God. - 1 Corinthians 1:18*

23   *For all the promises of God in him are yea, and in him Amen, unto the glory of God by us. - 2 Corinthians 1:20*

is found in the Word of God, the Lord Jesus Christ. And when we fail to receive Him, we fail to receive what is found in Him.[24]

Is God's Word, the Bible, eternal, infallible, and inerrant? Yes! Does the God of the Bible keep His promises? Yes! Does the God of the Bible answer prayer? Yes! How then can we experience the miraculous in our own lives? If God's power is available to us today as it was to those in former times, how do we access it? These are questions we will answer in the following pages.

JOURNALING TIPS

At the beginning of your journal you may wish to create a Table of Contents. First, decide on the divisions you want in your journal:

Promises
Prayer Requests
Prayers of Affirmation
Praise and Answers

List these divisions at the beginning of your journal. Decide how many pages you want to give each section. Flip to the first location and label it. Note the page number and record it in the Table of Contents. Repeat this for each section.

---

24   *For in him dwelleth all the fulness of the Godhead bodily. And ye are complete in him, which is the head of all principality and power: - Colossians 2:9-10*

Ye have not chosen me, but I have chosen you, and ordained you, that ye should go and bring forth fruit, and that your fruit should

remain:

that whatsoever ye shall ask of the Father in my name, he may give it you. - John 15:16

The Role of Prayer

WE MUST ASK TO RECEIVE

What must we do to have our prayers answered and see His promises fulfilled in our lives? Some feel that there must be a certain intensity in their prayers. Some suggest visualizing their prayer answered. Others teach that you must repeat your prayer day after day to receive your answer. Many excellent books have been written on the subject of prayer. They all teach one common message; to have our prayers answered, we must pray.

Ye lust, and have not: ye kill, and desire to have, and cannot obtain: ye fight and war, yet ye have not, because ye ask not. - James 4:2

When we are tempted to fret over a particular situation we should be reminded of James 4:2. Why would we expect to find an answer, if we have not asked? When we feel that we can handle a situation on our own, we rely on our own strength and wisdom to resolve it. Recognizing that God gives us that strength and wisdom, we often achieve outstanding results. It is when we forget God that frustration, anxiety, anger, and other dark emotions take over, and our results are anything but satisfactory.

We should all be keenly aware of our dependence upon God. A good friend works in finance where there are ample opportunities to make critical mistakes. When her day seems to be going awry, she is reminded to pray. She has avoided many frustrated hours trying to reconcile an account because she remembered to pray for His wisdom before she began the day. No matter where we work, we are all in need of God's wisdom day by day and moment by moment.[25] God promised us wisdom. Why would we not pray for that wisdom when we need it the most?

No matter how hurried we are, we should never begin a day without asking for God's help and direction. Whether we are working in a high pressure finance office or training our children at home, we cannot do the job He has given to us without Him. We are dependent upon Him and His promises for wisdom and strength.

Sensitivity to our needs and confidence in His promises should be enough to cause us to pray about everything, every day.[26]

WE MUST SEEK GOD'S WILL AND NOT OUR OWN

We can know the will of God in prayer. We often put an 'escape' clause into our
Before we can pray effectively we must first believe that Our God wants to answer our prayers.
prayers. We precede our requests with the phrase, "If it be your will . . ." Of course, praying in God's will is a prerequisite of answered prayer, but the truth behind our proviso is that we doubt that it is God's will to answer our prayers. Before we can pray effectively we must first believe that Our God **wants** to answer our prayers.

What possible reason could we have to pray if we did not believe that God wants to hear and answer our prayers? God's will is to provide for His children. Often, we pray, "If it be thy will," when He has already stated that it is His will to meet our needs. We

---

25   *If any of you lack wisdom, let him ask of God, that giveth to all men liberally, and upbraideth not; and it shall be given him. - James 1:5.*

26   *Pray without ceasing. - 1 Thessalonians 5:17*

insult our loving Father when we doubt His willingness to care for us. Consider Jesus' teaching in Luke 11 - *For every one that asketh receiveth; and he that seeketh findeth; and to him that knocketh it shall be opened. If a son shall ask bread of any of you that is a father, will he give him a stone? or if he ask a fish, will he for a fish give him a serpent? Or if he shall ask an egg, will he offer him a scorpion? If ye then, being evil, know how to give good gifts unto your children: how much more shall your heavenly Father give the Holy Spirit to them that ask him?* - Luke 11:10-13

We should come to God with the confidence of a child coming to his or her father. We should **know** that it pleases Our Father to hear from us and to answer us. This is not to say that children do not sometimes ask 'amiss'; sometimes children ask for things that are not good for them. A wise and loving parent does not grant such a request. The interesting thing about children is that they usually know when they are asking for things they should not have. So, do we! If we are not certain what God's will is concerning a particular situation, we have but to ask for His guidance.[27]

God loves us. God is pleased to give us not only our needs but many times our desires also. God granting us our desires is a result of a tender, trusting relationship.[28] If we are sensitive to the will of God and submissive to His Spirit, we can trust Him to deliver us from selfish desires that would prevent us from performing His will! We must pray in God's will, by faith believing that God hears and answers. The more we delight in Him, the more we come to realize our truest desires and our prayers become less about ourselves and more about His will.

> *God is pleased to give us not only our needs but many times our desires also. God granting us our desires is a result of a tender, trusting relationship.*

WE MUST ASK EXPECTANTLY

We stop asking when we do not recognize and appreciate God's answers, and when we give ourselves the credit for what God has done. Some men are described as "self-made." None of us is self-made! Only in pride and arrogance do we credit ourselves

---

27   *And this is the confidence that we have in him, that, if we ask any thing according to his will, he heareth us: And if we know that he hear us, whatsoever we ask, we know that we have the petitions that we desired of him.* - 1 John 5:14-15

28   *Delight thyself also in the LORD; and he shall give thee the desires of thine heart. Psalm 37:4*

with what God has done, is doing, and will do. The psalmist said it this way, *"Know ye that the LORD he is God: it is he that hath made us, and not we ourselves; we are his people, and the sheep of his pasture."* - Psalm 100:3

If someone prays for the sun to come up in the morning, is it an answer to prayer when the sun comes up? Real prayer is asking God to do something that only He can do. We may be afraid to pray for things only God can do. This is the true test of faith and reliance in and on the God of our Salvation. Just because something is impossible does not mean it is not God's will. It may require prayer and fasting. It may mean persistent, consistent prayer.[29]

The promise of answered prayer lies with the children of God, although God can and in some cases does hear and answer the prayers of the unsaved. In Job 21:14-16. Job explains to his companions that the wicked have no regard for God and no need for prayer, having no confidence in God.[30] The believer when asked, "…what profit should we have, if we pray unto him?" can respond **unlimited!**

The following are a few examples of those who prayed in faith believing and the resulting answers to their prayers.

MOSES PRAYED FOR ISRAEL.

And now, I beseech thee, let the power of my Lord be great, according as thou hast spoken, saying, The LORD is longsuffering, and of great mercy, forgiving iniquity and transgression, and by no means clearing the guilty, visiting the iniquity of the fathers upon the children unto the third and fourth generation. Pardon, I beseech thee, the iniquity of this people according unto the greatness of thy mercy, and as thou hast forgiven this people, from Egypt even until now. And the LORD said, I have pardoned according to thy word: But as truly as I live, all the earth shall be filled with the glory of the LORD. - Numbers 14:17-21

---

29   *But Jesus beheld them, and said unto them, With men this is impossible; but with God all things are possible. - Matthew 19:26 and he said, The things which are impossible with men are possible with God. - Luke 18:27*

30   *Therefore they say unto God, Depart from us; for we desire not the knowledge of thy ways. What is the Almighty, that we should serve him? and what profit should we have, if we pray unto him? Lo, their good is not in their hand: the counsel of the wicked is far from me. - Job 21:14-16*

Samson prayed when he thirsted and was given water from the jawbone of an ass.
And he was sore athirst, and called on the LORD, and said, Thou hast given this great deliverance into the hand of thy servant: and now shall I die for thirst, and fall into the hand of the uncircumcised? But God clave an hollow place that was in the jaw, and there came water thereout; and when he had drunk, his spirit came again, and he revived: wherefore he called the name thereof Enhakkore, which is in Lehi unto this day. - Judges 15:18-19

Hannah prayed for a son and was given Samuel.
For this child I prayed; and the LORD hath given me my petition which I asked of him: - 1 Samuel 1:27

Solomon prayed for wisdom.
Give therefore thy servant an understanding heart to judge thy people, that I may discern between good and bad: for who is able to judge this thy so great a people? ... Behold, I have done according to thy words: lo, I have given thee a wise and an understanding heart; so that there was none like thee before thee, neither after thee shall any arise like unto thee. - 1 Kings 3:9, 12

Elijah prayed and called fire down.
And it came to pass at the time of the offering of the evening sacrifice, that Elijah the prophet came near, and said, LORD God of Abraham, Isaac, and of Israel, let it be known this day that thou art God in Israel, and that I am thy servant, and that I have done all these things at thy word. Hear me, O LORD, hear me, that this people may know that thou art the LORD God, and that thou hast turned their heart back again. Then the fire of the LORD fell, and consumed the burnt sacrifice, and the wood, and the stones, and the dust, and licked up the water that was in the trench. And when all the people saw it, they fell on their faces: and they said, The LORD, he is the God; the LORD, he is the God. - 1 Kings 18:36-39

Hezekiah prayed for deliverance from the enemy.
Now therefore, O LORD our God, I beseech thee, save thou us out of his hand, that all the kingdoms of the earth may know that thou art the LORD God, even thou only. Then Isaiah the son of Amoz sent to Hezekiah, saying, Thus saith the LORD God of Israel, That which thou hast prayed to me against Sennacherib king of Assyria I have heard. - 2 Kings 19:19-20

The list goes on and on: Nehemiah in Nehemiah 4:9, David in Psalm 18:6, Jeremiah in Lamentations 3:55, Daniel in Daniel 9:20, Jonah in Jonah 2:2-10, Zacharias in Luke 1:13, the blind man, the thief on cross, the Apostles, Cornelius, Paul in prison, and the Lord Jesus Himself, all PRAYED! And God answered!

Psalm 91 is known as the Soldiers' Psalm. According to accounts, a laminated copy of the printed Psalm was given to soldiers as early as World War I. Soldiers deployed in the Middle East also kept copies of the Psalm with them. They would recite it often, trusting God's promise to be with them in the battles they faced. The final verses read – *Because he hath set his love upon me, therefore will I deliver him: I will set him on high, because he hath known my name. He shall call upon me, and I will answer him: I will be with him in trouble; I will deliver him, and honour him. With long life will I satisfy him, and shew him my salvation.* - Psalm 91:14-16

As a child of God we can be assured that when we call, He hears! He hears because or our relationship with Him. This Psalm speaks of a loving relationship. We are His dear children. We KNOW Him.

We Must Pray in Faith[31]

There are two qualifiers for answered prayer.

There are two qualifiers for answered prayer. The first is believing that God is. We could elaborate by saying that we must believe that God is Who He says He is. God is love. God is merciful. God is gracious. God is faithful. God is unchanging. God is mighty in strength and wisdom. God is able. God draws near to us when we draw near to Him. Sometimes our prayers are hindered because we do not believe in Who God is. The second qualifier is believing that God is willing and able to answer our prayers. Sometimes our prayers are hindered because we do not believe God keeps all of His promises.

When we trustingly ask as little children, we are confident our Father:
    1) has the resources to grant our requests
    2) is ready and willing to grant our requests

---

31   *But without faith it is impossible to please him: for he that cometh to God must believe that he is, and that he is a rewarder of them that diligently seek him.* - Hebrews 11:6

OVERCOMING ANXIETY & WORRY

Do you struggle with anxiety? Call it stress, call it worry, call it fear, call it nervousness, we all deal with it in some form or another. Some people experience greater feelings of anxiety than others, but all of us deal with some anxiety at some point in our lives. Have you ever laid awake at night reliving feelings of embarrassment over something you did or said? Do you find yourself obsessing over what 'might' happen in the future? As hard as we try, we cannot avoid all problems or prepare for every possible difficulty that may come our way. The issue is not if we will experience anxiety but rather how we will choose to deal with it.

Anxiety and worry will overcome us, if we do not address the sources and take action to alleviate them. All of humanity wrestles with guilt. None of us has lived a sinless life and the longer we live the more our sins and failures mount up. God knew our greatest need was that of forgiveness and He provided this through His Son's death on the cross. Jesus Christ is the only source of true and total forgiveness. When we diligently seek Him, we find the forgiveness we so desperately need. Freedom from guilt and shame eliminates this great burden of anxiety most people bear.

Young people often worry about what others think of them. They struggle for acceptance and approval. The answer is not found in the love and acceptance of one's peers but rather in the unconditional love of our God. This is not to say that as Christians we do not care about our relationship with others, but we seek the favor of God above all others. He is the rewarder of those who diligently seek Him!

LACK OF TIME & MONEY

Two more common sources of stress in our lives are not having enough time and not having enough money. Learning to budget our time and our money addresses two key areas of anxiety in most of our lives. Still there are times when we are faced with the unexpected. When our resources are depleted, we have a Heavenly Father willing and able to meet our every need.

Praying in faith is the antidote for anxiety. Asking specifically for our own needs settles our hearts and minds. 1 Peter 5:7 tells us to cast **all** of our cares on Him[32]

---

32   *Casting all your care upon him; for he careth for you. 1 Peter 5:7*

If we are praying in faith expecting God to answer our prayers, why would we not give Him **all** of our concerns and worries? What would our lives be like if we simply had no worries whatsoever? Isn't that what we are commanded to do?[33]

Christians should enjoy the security of knowing God takes care of them regardless of their circumstances.

A Christian should be remarkable in the calm and contentment they exhibit. Jesus said that those in the world are the ones who must concern themselves with having their needs met. Christians should enjoy the security of knowing God takes care of them regardless of their circumstances.

It is not always God's will to deliver us out of our trials. There are times when we are called upon by faith to glorify God in the midst of our trials. God always keeps His promises and God always answers prayer, but always in His own timing and in His own way and always for our good and His glory.

Hebrews 11 is known as the 'Faith Hall of Fame'. It begins, *Now faith is the substance of things hoped for, the evidence of things not seen.* - Hebrews 11:1 In the verses that follow we read of the miraculous deliverance men and women experienced "by faith".[34] But as we read further we find that others who rather than being delivered from their trials, endured the cruelty of men. God's promises of deliverance for them were yet to come.[35]

We must <u>not</u> allow our fears or uncertainties to hamper our asking or believing that God hears and answers our prayers. Answers to specific prayers encourages our faith and motivates us to ask for even greater things. God is glorified when we ask in faith specifically.

---

33   *Be careful for nothing; but in every thing by prayer and supplication with thanksgiving let your requests be made known unto God.* - Philippians 4:6

34   *Who through faith subdued kingdoms, wrought righteousness, obtained promises, stopped the mouths of lions,* - Hebrews 11:33

35   *And others had trial of cruel mockings and scourgings, yea, moreover of bonds and imprisonment: ... And these all, having obtained a good report through faith, received not the promise: God having provided some better thing for us, that they without us should not be made perfect.* - Hebrews 11:36, 39-40

We all experience need. The need may be others' or our own. Need is what almost always drives us to seek God in prayer. If we do not recognize our need, we do not pray. Job recognized the need of his children and prayed for them before a greater need arose. There are many substantial needs that we don't always recognize.

We need wisdom and not earthly wisdom; we need the wisdom that comes only from above. God knows what we do not know. God sees what we do not see. We desperately need His wisdom in every area of our lives. *For wisdom is better than rubies; and all the things that may be desired are not to be compared to it.* - Proverbs 8:11

We have physical needs. We need safety, shelter, clothing, and, of course, food. In a society with food in abundance and a myriad of social programs to assist the needy our tendency is to ignore God as the source of the many benefits we enjoy.

Asking is the key to having our needs met. Jesus taught us two points concerning our physical needs. First, that God knows our needs before we ask, *"... for your Father knoweth what things ye have need of, before ye ask him."* - Matthew 6:8. And second, that we are to ask that those needs be met, *"Give us this day our daily bread."* - Matthew 6:11. Asking reminds us that God is the source of even our most basic needs.

JOURNALING TIPS

Make it Personal!

It helps to keep a prayer journal. Writing down our specific prayers allows us to note God's specific answers. Sometimes we may be tempted to think an answer to prayer was 'coincidental.' The more specific a prayer request is, the less likely the answer is merely a coincidence and the greater the glory to God!

It is important to know God answers prayer, but it is even more important to know **God answers my prayers!**

For we are his
workmanship,
created in Christ Jesus unto good works, which God
hath before ordained that we should walk in them. - Ephesians 2:10

The Divine Purpose

The promises of God have a purpose! They are intended for our profit. It is God's plan that we profit from His promises.

Have you ever felt like you must "talk" God into answering your prayers and fulfilling His promises? This is not the case! God finds pleasure in fulfilling His promises in our lives. *Having predestinated us unto the adoption of children by Jesus Christ to himself, according to the good pleasure of his will,* - Ephesians 1:5

God is purposing all things in us for His "good pleasure" according to His plan. God's purpose is that His will is fulfilled through us for His "good pleasure".

For it is God which worketh in you both to will and to do of his good pleasure.
- Philippians 2:13

God created all things including man for His good pleasure. This was the purpose of creation.[36]

It pleased God to promise His people whatever He wanted for them.[37] His will is that we might profit from His promises according to His plan. Our profiting from His promises provides Him with pleasure. This is the purpose in God's promises!

One of the great joys of cooking is serving a delicious meal to others and watching them enjoy it. The cook had a plan and a purpose, and it was to provide enjoyment to others. The cook's pleasure comes from the appreciation of the meal.

Parents also understand the pleasure of meeting the desires of a child. I am really not sure who derives the most enjoyment on Christmas mornings - the children who excitedly open the gifts from under the tree, or the parents who carefully chose and wrapped those gifts with each child in mind.

God's Purpose is Seen Through a Favored People

I had a good friend who liked to say, "I am God's favorite!" We would all then say, "No, I am God's favorite!" And of course, there always was someone who took everything literally who would say, "God doesn't have any favorites!" It is true that God is no respecter of persons, but He does show favor to His people.[38] As Ruth and Esther found favor in the eyes of earthly kings. God's children are meant to live in God's favor.

God has Provided Abundantly

There are many things God wants for us. God has provided abundantly for His children. Would a child on Christmas morning refuse to open a gift addressed to him?

---

36   *Thou art worthy, O Lord, to receive glory and honour and power: for thou hast created all things, and for thy pleasure they are and were created. - Revelation 4:11*

37   *Declaring the end from the beginning, and from ancient times the things that are not yet done, saying, My counsel shall stand, and I will do all my pleasure: - Isaiah 46:10*

38   *And the angel came in unto her, and said, Hail, thou that art highly favoured, the Lord is with thee: blessed art thou among women. - Luke 1:28*

Would she ignore a brightly colored package labeled with her name? Of course not! Children eagerly await the opening of those packages. The days before are filled with anticipation and wonder. So much so, that some have been known to shake and even peek inside their gifts ahead of time.

Knowing that God has promised us the desires of our hearts, why do we not live expectantly? Why are we not excited over the things God has in store for us?[39]

Could it be that we doubt God's promises? Do we fail to seek God's blessings because we do not appreciate or understand the purpose of His promises? Satan's lie to Eve was that God was not good because God was keeping good things from her. We like to think we could not be so easily deceived, but do we sincerely believe that God's plan and purpose for us is for our good and His glory?

What hinders our faith in God's goodness? Feelings. Feelings are not based on promises. *Feelings are not based on promises. Feelings are based on the physical. Faith based on feelings always fails.* Feelings are based on the physical. One day we can get out of bed, see the sun shining, hear the birds singing, smell the coffee brewing, and look forward to a great day based solely upon our feelings. The very next day we may crawl out of bed with a headache, see the rain clouds, hear the kids arguing, and smell the toast burning, and look with dread toward lousy day. We based our expectations on our feelings and we based our feelings on the physical world around us. Faith based on feelings always fails.

JOURNALING TIPS

Prayers of affirmation are prayers based upon promise we claim personally. They affirm God's promises to us. Writing these in your journal and then reading them out loud impacts our mind and spirit.

"God is working in me for His good pleasure."Philippians 2:13
"God is caring for me today." I Peter 5:7
"Because I delight in HIm, God is giving me the desires of my heart." Psalm 34:7

---

39   Jesus asked, *If ye then, being evil, know how to give good gifts unto your children, how much more shall your Father which is in heaven give good things to them that ask him? - Matthew 7:11*

And whatsoever we ask,
we receive of him,
because we keep his commandments, and do those things
that are pleasing in his sight.

- 1 John 3:22

The Essential Principles

There are two principle truths concerning God's promises that we cannot ignore if we are to take full advantage of them and find their profit.

If God said it, He will perform it. If God said it, then it is recorded in the Bible, God's written Word! If it is a promise of God, it is pictured in Scripture. God's covenant promises to Noah in Genesis 9:8-16 and to Abram in Genesis 12:2-3 and to David in 2 Samuel 7:1-16 have never failed. Much of what God promised in the Old Testament has already been fulfilled. We can see God keeps His promises!

God keeps His promises as is evidenced by the promise He made to Abraham and Sarah, that in their old age they would have a son. Romans 4 says of Abraham's faith, *Who against hope believed in hope, that he might become the father of many nations, according to that which was spoken, So shall thy seed be. And being not weak in faith, he considered not his own body now dead, when he was about an hundred years old, neither yet the deadness of Sara's womb:* - Romans 4:18-19. Isaac, the seed of promise, was born and Abraham's faith in God's promise was rewarded. In like manner so are we when we, by faith, believe God's promises unto salvation!

Every promise of God is from His Word. The word promise describes a pledge which obligates one to another to complete or satisfy an agreement. The word promise is used hundreds of times in Scripture, "promise!"

There are other terms implying this same thought. The Hebrew word in the Old Testament, Dahtar, is often translated 'word'. We see it translated 'promise' in 1 Kings. *Blessed be the LORD, that hath given rest unto his people Israel, according to all that he promised: there hath not failed one word of all his good promise, which he promised by the hand of Moses his servant.* - 1 Kings 8:56. We would say of a man, "He gave me his word ", meaning "He gave me his promise." In God's case, His Word is His Promise. This is true with God, but not so much with men.

Another Hebrew term translated 'promise' is Omer. Omer is also often translated 'saying'. *Is his mercy clean gone for ever? doth his promise fail for evermore?* - Psalm 77:8. In the New Testament a promise is many times referred to as a faithful saying. *This is a faithful saying and worthy of all acceptation.* - 1 Timothy 4:9

God is faithful. His promises are predicated on the precept of His Word. Over and over again we are reminded that God is faithful. His promises are predicated on the precept of His Word. If you are tempted to question or doubt His promises, consider these verses.

Let us hold fast the profession of our faith without wavering; (for he is faithful that promised;) - Hebrews 10:23

Through faith also Sara herself received strength to conceive seed, and was delivered of a child when she was past age, because she judged him faithful who had promised. - Hebrews 11:11

God cannot Lie.[40] What God has promised He will do.[41] Pilate asked Jesus this question, "What is truth?" Pilate, like all men without God, had no assurance in himself. Truth for him was relative and ever changing. And yet before Pilate that selfsame day stood the very truth of God incarnate in the person of the Lord Jesus Christ, Who declared, *I am the way, the truth, and the life: no man cometh unto the Father, but by me.* - John 14:6.

His promises to us are based upon the absolute dependability of His Word. Is it any wonder that true freedom is only found in knowing the Word of God?[42] Jesus revealed, while praying to His Father, *thy word is truth.* - John 17:17

God is faithful.[43] Referring to Abraham, we understand that his faith was based upon his knowledge of God and His Word. *He staggered not at the promise of God through unbelief; but was strong in faith, giving glory to God; And being fully persuaded that, what he had promised, he was able also to perform.* - Romans 4:20-21

His will, His plan, and His purpose are all for His pleasure, and rightly so!

We can trust our faithful God and His Word to us. The Word of God cannot fail. It never has. It never will, not a jot not a tittle. God's promises are sure! And God gives us His promises for our profit and for His good pleasure; it is God's plan and God's purpose in giving and keeping His promises to us.

God is faithful, by whom ye were called unto the fellowship of his Son Jesus Christ our Lord. - 1 Corinthians 1:9

Faithful is he that calleth you, who also will do it. - 1 Thessalonians 5:24

---

40 *That by two immutable things, in which it was impossible for God to lie, we might have a strong consolation, who have fled for refuge to lay hold upon the hope set before us: - Hebrews 6:18*

41 *In hope of eternal life, which God, that cannot lie, promised before the world began; - Titus 1:2*

42 *And ye shall know the truth, and the truth shall make you free. - John 8:32*

43 *It is of the LORD'S mercies that we are not consumed, because his compassions fail not. They are new every morning: great is thy faithfulness. - Lamentations 3:22-23*

Linda, who trusted explicitly in God and His promises, boldly joined a group headed to Mexico City. Here's her testimony of God's faithfulness to her.

"I was on a mission's trip to Mexico City to hand out a million tracts in a week. An amazing project to be a part of.

I was part of the group that made the lunches each day for our team. We needed to buy some additional groceries and unfortunately had not been able to get to the store until about 1:00 in the morning. After locating a Volkswagen taxi, (we learned that Mexico City is where all of the Volkswagens from America retire) off to the store we went.

When we got to the store we divided the grocery list between us and headed off to find our assigned items. Since everything was labeled in Spanish, we had to search by pictures for what looked like it might be close to what we needed. I was looking for a particular item, looking up scanning the products, and not paying attention to the floor.

As I was walking hurriedly down an aisle, I felt myself slipping suddenly backwards as if my feet were going out from under me. At that exact moment it felt as if someone put their hands on my back and was keeping me upright. I turned and saw a slippery mess . . . someone had dropped and broken a jar. Mayonnaise with broken shards of glass were splashed across the floor. If I had fallen backwards, I would not only have hit my head on the floor but would have also fallen on all the broken glass that was about head level.

I know that the Lord sent one of His angels to keep me standing upright because there could be no other reason why I did not actually fall.

Back home, individuals volunteered to be our prayer partners. Taking turns, members our church family in the United States, formed a 24 hour-a-day prayer chain. On this particular night, the man praying was particularly impressed to pray for me. At the exact moment I began to fall, he was asking God to protect me. He could have assumed that I would already be in bed and asleep and not prayed for my safety. He was faithful and obedient to do his part in praying for me and the Lord was faithful to answer that prayer.

The Lord is faithful to care for us even when we don't realize our impending need. I am very grateful for the prayers of one man in particular and the answered prayers from our mighty, faithful God."

EVERY PROMISE GIVEN TO US IS CONDITIONAL

One word that often precedes a promise is '**if**'; 'if' is followed by terms and conditions and then followed by a promise. This is known as a conditional statement or an 'if/then statement'. A good example of this is found in 2 Chronicles 7:14 ***If** my people, which are called by my name, shall humble themselves, and pray, and seek my face, **and** turn from their wicked ways; **then** will I hear from heaven, and will forgive their sin, and will heal their land.*

We also frequently find a promise in a compound sentence where a condition is linked to a promise by the conjunction 'and'. An example of this can be found in Matthew 11:28 & 29 *Come unto me, all ye that labour and are heavy laden, **and** I will give you rest. Take my yoke upon you, and learn of me; for I am meek and lowly in heart: **and** ye shall find rest unto your souls.*

God wants us to come to Him, to call upon Him, to claim His promises, so He can profit us for His good pleasure! Remember it's His plan and it's His purpose, that we come to Him.

There are hundreds of these conditional promises given to us by God in His Word! As you note God's promises in your journal, be careful to also note the condition attached to the promise. Study the following verses noting the condition and the promise that follows. As a help we have underlined the conjunctions.

*Call unto me, **and** I will answer thee, and shew thee great and mighty things, which thou knowest not.* - Jeremiah 33:3

*Ask, **and** it shall be given you; seek, **and** ye shall find; knock, **and** it shall be opened unto you:* - Matthew 7:7

***If** any of you lack wisdom, let him ask of God, that giveth to all men liberally, and upbraideth not; **and** it shall be given him.* - James 1:5

It's God's Word! He has promised! Every promise of God is predicated upon a precept (God's Word). If He said it, He will perform it, we have His Word on it.

Delight thyself also in the LORD; **and** *he shall give thee the desires of thine heart.* - Psalm 37:4

What is our part in this verse? To delight. What is God's part? To give us our desires. Now underline the condition and the corresponding promise as you see here.

Delight *thyself also in the Lord;* **and** *he shall give thee the* **desires** *of thine heart.*

As we delight and put Him first, God will not only grant us the desires of our heart, but He will place the right desires into our hearts. Our part? The delighting. God's part? The desires.

We are to delight in Him - that is, to put Him first, which Jesus taught was the first and great commandment. *Jesus said unto him, Thou shalt love the Lord thy God with all thy heart, and with all thy soul, and with all thy mind.* - Matthew 22:37

We might label this related verse "Seeking and Supplying". It is found in Matthew 6:33, *But seek ye first the kingdom of God, and his righteousness;* **and** *all these things shall be added unto you.* - Matthew 6:33. We see here the promise that '*all these things shall be added unto you.* Here, again we find the conjunction 'and' dividing the condition from the promise. When we put God and His righteousness first, God supplies all of our needs.

We could label this next promise "Declaring and Directing". This often quoted example is found in Proverbs 3:5-6. *Trust in the LORD with all thine heart; and lean not unto thine own understanding. In all thy ways acknowledge him,* **and** *he shall direct thy paths.* - Proverbs 3:5-6

Our part is to obey Him. God's part is to prosper us.

Our part is the declaring. Acknowledging God in everything! God's Part is the directing our path. If you're not doing your part, you may be missing out on God's doing His part! If you're not doing your part, you may not be going in the right direction!

Now let's consider Isaiah 1:19. **If** *ye be willing and obedient, ye shall eat the good of the land:* - Isaiah 1:19

Our part is to obey Him. God's part is to prosper us. God called the land of Israel a land of milk and honey. There, grapes grew in abundance. It was a rich and prosperous land, much like our own nation. When a nation or a person obeys God, He prospers them.

God promises to give us good things. God promises to bless our labors. But, there are conditions to these promises.

Here are a few more promises to add to your journal. We could label this next promise "Relying and Resting".

*Take my yoke upon you, and learn of me; for I am meek and lowly in heart: **and** ye shall find rest unto your souls.* - Matthew 11:29 God promises to lighten our load if we will simply come to Jesus, trusting His Word.

We could label the following promise "Giving and Getting".

Bring ye all the tithes into the storehouse, that there may be meat in mine house, and prove me now herewith, saith the LORD of hosts, if I will not open you the windows of heaven, and pour you out a blessing, that there shall not be room enough to receive it. - Malachi 3:10

When we do our part, God will do His part. What are we willing to do with God's promises? God's promises cannot fail. His part is proven over and over by generations of believers. Are we proving God's promises true? If not, sin may be robbing us of our many blessings. Sin hardens our hearts and clouds our spiritual discernment. Sin dulls our sensitivity to the Holy Spirit. Sin drowns out the voice of God. James does tell us that we have not because we ask not, but he goes on to say that we also have not because we ask amiss. *Ye ask, and receive not, because ye ask amiss, that ye may consume it upon your lusts.* - James 4:3

If our prayers are going unanswered, we need a spiritual check-up. Spending time in prayer confessing our sin and recognizing our need heightens our awareness of the presence of God and His leading. The more aware we are of God's presence the more sensitive we are to our own sin.

Another wonderful promise of God to meet our need of forgiveness is found in 1 John. We could label this promise "Confess and Cleanse". *If we confess our sins, he is faithful and just to forgive us our sins, and to cleanse us from all unrighteousness.* - 1 John 1:9

What areas of concern do you carry today? Health, family, finances, church, future, friends, parents, job, car, missions, ministry, home, mate, children? When the many uses for smart phones and tablets were being introduced, one savvy advertising firm came up with the slogan, "There's an app for that!" A Christians response to a need might well be, "There's a promise for that!" Is your concern for finances? There's a promise for that! Is your concern for your future? There's a promise for that! Is your concern for your job? Is your concern for health? There's a promise for that!

There are two truths we must always remember concerning the promises of God
> 1. All the promises God gives to us are conditional.
> 2. The first condition is believing.

JOURNALING TIPS

As you record promises in your journal, be sure to also record God's fulfillment of those promises. This will help to remind you that God is faithful. He always keeps His promises. Looking back over your journal will remind you of how faithful God has been in your life. There will be times when we fail God because we are human, but your journal will be yet another evidence that God never fails us!

We do not have to understand God's promises. We only have to believe them as the old song by Daniel W. Whittle so wonderfully illustrates.

I know Whom I have Believed

I know not why God's wondrous grace
To me He hath made known,
Nor why, unworthy, Christ in love
Redeemed me for His own.

Refrain:
But "I know Whom I have believed,
And am persuaded that He is able
To keep that which I've committed
Unto Him against that day."

I know not how this saving faith
To me He did impart,
Nor how believing in His Word
Wrought peace within my heart.

I know not how the Spirit moves,
Convincing men of sin,
Revealing Jesus through the Word,
Creating faith in Him.

I know not when my Lord may come,
At night or noonday fair,
Nor if I walk the vale with Him,
Or meet Him in the air.

Daniel W. Whittle, pub.1883

The LORD is my strength and my shield; my heart trusted in him, and I am *helped:* therefore my heart greatly rejoiceth; and with my song will I praise him.

- Psalm 28:7

The Response of Praise

512 times the Bible commands "Praise the Lord" in some variation. That does not include all of the times we are commanded to rejoice, give thanks, sing, or make a joyful noise unto the Lord. Almost always these commands are in relation to the wonderful works of the Lord. Here are just three examples out of hundreds.

Oh that men would praise the LORD for his goodness, and for his wonderful works to the children of men! - Psalm 107:8

O sing unto the LORD a new song; for he hath done marvellous things: his right hand, and his holy arm, hath gotten him the victory. - Psalm 98:1

Praise ye the LORD. O give thanks unto the LORD; for he is good: for his mercy endureth for ever. - Psalm 106:1

We Must See God

As human beings our vision is limited. Paul said that *now we see through a glass darkly and only know in part.* - I Corinthians 13:12. But around the throne of God in heaven, where He is seen as He is, there is continual praise. *And I beheld, and I heard the voice of many angels round about the throne and the beasts and the elders: and the number of them was ten thousand times ten thousand, and thousands of thousands; Saying with a loud voice, Worthy is the Lamb that was slain to receive power, and riches, and wisdom, and strength, and honour, and glory, and blessing.* - Revelation 5:11-12

The world around us can easily be a distraction. We tend to focus on our perceptions and not upon His promises. When we take our eyes off of our circumstances and look toward His sufficiency, our faith and trust in all He has promised grows. *Lift up your eyes on high, and behold who hath created these things, that bringeth out their host by number: he calleth them all by names by the greatness of his might, for that he is strong in power; not one faileth.* - Isaiah 40:26

Like Peter, the waves and wind and storms of life hold our attention. We take our eyes off of the Master and spend our time focusing on the mayhem around us. We should rather be *Looking unto Jesus the author and finisher of our faith;* - Hebrews 12:2 Then, and only then, can He take hold and lift us out of our turmoil. When we see Him, we rejoice. *For our heart shall rejoice in him, because we have trusted in his holy name.* - Psalm 33:21

The Psalmist encourages us to trust Him and to experience His goodness. *O taste and see that the LORD is good: blessed is the man that trusteth in him.* - Psalm 34:8

Many women long and pray to become mothers. Some never do conceive, while others experience heartbreaking miscarriages. It is not that God does not answer their prayers, but rather that He answers in ways we do not expect. We choose our response to these situations. We can become bitter and disillusioned or we can trust and praise our loving Father. Here is the touching testimony of one woman who chose to trust and praise Him!

"One thing the Lord has shown me, especially over the last 15 years or so, is that He gives grace to accept His answer, even when it's not what we prayed for. He has shown His love for me over and over; how can I think He doesn't want the absolute best for me? How can I question Him? However- it's easy to say that, it's a lot more difficult to remember when you lose the baby you've prayed so fervently for. And when it happens again, it's even harder.

I've seen God answer so many prayers in my personal life, it's one of the many great aspects of being saved at a young age and growing up with Him as my heavenly Father. When my daughter was born 14 weeks early, even after fervent prayer that she wouldn't come so early, God gave us the grace to handle the long journey in the hospital. When she needed a minor (but still scary!) heart procedure done at three weeks, weighing just three pounds, God gave us the strength and peace to get through it. When she came home on oxygen and a heart monitor, He gave us the knowledge and understanding to be her caretakers, and strengthened our marriage, truly making us partners. And now, sixteen years later, with a healthy teenager with absolutely no long-term complications from her prematurity, we get to see those answers to prayers every single day.

I've also seen God answer prayers in a way that seemed to make no sense. In my weakest moments of faith, I took them as unanswered prayer. How could it be God's will that my perfect baby was delivered too early to be viable? Wasn't it His will for us to have more children? We were raising our family in a Godly home, with a church that loved the Lord and sought daily to do His will and further His work. Why couldn't we have this baby? God taught me that it's in these times that you truly feel His presence, His peace, and His comfort even in the midst of heartbreak. So when, a few years down the road, we lost our son midway through the second trimester, we knew God would be our source of comfort. It was, of course, still completely heart-breaking, and we definitely struggled and spent many nights crying out to God, but we also knew from experience how much we could lean on Him. It brought us even closer together as a family, and we grew to know God in a way we hadn't before. The sting is always there; when we lose a loved one, there's always an ache left behind, but we cling to the hope God's given us. So, even when we have to accept that we may never know "why" prayers are answered the way they are, we can rest in the promise that He only wants what's best for us, and that He loves our little ones even more than we do."

This young woman's faith and trust in God has opened many doors as she ministers to others who have also experienced the heartbreak of miscarriage. She sees God working in her life and using her on a daily basis! Praise is the result of seeing God. Praise is the logical response to God's goodness and greatness. Praise attributes to God the glory He is due. *By him therefore let us offer the sacrifice of praise to God continually, that is, the fruit of our lips giving thanks to his name.* - Hebrews 13:15

WE MUST REMEMBER GOD'S GREATNESS

As human beings our vision is not only limited, but so is our memory. We need to practice remembering all that God has done for us. This is where a journal is so very useful. Writing down and documenting God's answers to our prayers reminds us of all the promises He has kept to us. It builds our faith and allows us to live a life of trust.

Remember the former things of old: for I am God, and there is none else; I am God, and there is none like me, - Isaiah 46:9

Memorial Day and Veterans Day are days our nation has set a side to simply remember what has been done for us by others. Thanksgiving Day is also meant as a time to remember and give thanks for the many blessings God has given to this nation. When we need God, we remember Him but, we should remember Him and His goodness to us always! Every day should be a day of remembrance and thanksgiving. *Bless the LORD, O my soul, and forget not all his benefits:* - Psalm 103:2

Worries and anxiety often visit us in the dark hours of the night. These are exactly the times we should remember the Lord and praise Him for His greatness. *My soul shall be satisfied as with marrow and fatness; and my mouth shall praise thee with joyful lips: When I remember thee upon my bed, and meditate on thee in the night watches. Because thou hast been my help, therefore in the shadow of thy wings will I rejoice.* - Psalm 63:5-7

Are you worried? Are you anxious? Are you apprehensive? Are you troubled? Stop and remember how God has cared for you in the past. Meditate on His ability to protect and care for you now. Rejoice in His promises to shield you from danger.

Do you remember a time when God's immeasurable power and unfathomable wisdom were particularly evident in your life? Perhaps you were awed by the crash of thunder during a storm. Perhaps you stood beside a mighty ocean or gazed at the night sky filled with stars and were overwhelmed with awe and wonder? And then you stopped and considered that He is our mighty God, that He cares for us, and that He sent His Son to die for us? These are times when praise must erupt from our hearts and lips. These are the times when the words to the old Swedish hymn, George Beverly Shea made famous, come to mind.

WE MUST THINK OF GOD'S GOODNESS

Then they that feared the LORD spake often one to another: and the LORD hearkened, and heard it, and a book of remembrance was written before him for them that feared the LORD, and that thought upon his name. - Malachi 3:16

Researchers tell us that we have thought patterns. Our thoughts then impact our attitudes. What many people do not realize is that thoughts and attitudes are a choice; we can choose the things we dwell upon, and we can choose to have an attitude of gratitude.

Finally, brethren, whatsoever things are true, whatsoever things are honest, whatsoever things are just, whatsoever things are pure, whatsoever things are lovely, whatsoever things are of good report; if there be any virtue, and if there be any praise, think on these things. - Philippians 4:8

Memorizing God's Word fills our minds with the right thoughts. We all know people who continually dwell on the negative. Their minds are filled with dark and discouraging thoughts, they continually remember the faults and sins of the world around them, and they live in fear of what may lie ahead. The Word of God is the antidote for these negative thinking patterns.

What time I am afraid, I will trust in thee. In God I will praise his word, in God I have put my trust; I will not fear what flesh can do unto me. - Psalm 56:3-4

"Think yourself thankful" is excellent advice, and our journals are a good place to start. Looking back over God's answers to our prayers and the fulfillment of His promises to us will give us much for which to be thankful. What we think about is what we talk about; when our thoughts are focused on the goodness of God and His grace and mercy to us, praise will be the result. *A good man out of the good treasure of his heart bringeth forth that which is good; and an evil man out of the evil treasure of his heart bringeth forth that which is evil: for of the abundance of the heart his mouth speaketh.* - Luke 6:45

The words we use are a result of the condition of our hearts and our minds. We are told to protect our hearts and our thinking.[44] The Bible calls our words "the fruit of our lips."[45] The thoughts we allow to be planted in our hearts and the thoughts we nurture and cultivate in our thinking produce the words we speak. In the book of Romans, Paul lists the words of the mouth as one of the key distinctions of unregenerate man. *Whose mouth is full of cursing and bitterness:* - Romans 3:14

Darlene had a great family, a good job, and attended a thriving church. She had many friends and participated in several ministries, but Darlene wasn't happy. Darlene constantly found fault with things and situations around her. She especially found fault with herself. She surrounded herself with others who were also critical and judgmental. She thought that she was just being honest and helping to improve the world around her.

At a women's conference Darlene attended, she was challenged to go one day without saying one negative word. Up until this experience, Darlene did not recognize how very negative her thoughts and words really were or how little time she spent being thankful. She did not see her negativity as sin until the Holy Spirit convicted and challenged her.

Darlene later shared with us how difficult it was to cut out her negative speech and thought patterns. It was very easy for her to slip back into the old habits. As soon as she realized where her words and thoughts were going, she had to confess them as sin and ask for God's help and forgiveness. Darlene said that a key to her victory over these negative thoughts and words was replacing them with praise.

He is thy praise, and he is thy God, that hath done for thee these great and terrible things, which thine eyes have seen. - Deuteronomy 10:21

---

44   *Keep thy heart with all diligence; for out of it are the issues of life. Put away from thee a froward mouth, and perverse lips put far from thee.* - Proverbs 4:23-24

45   *By him therefore let us offer the sacrifice of praise to God continually, that is, the fruit of our lips giving thanks to his name.* - Hebrews 13:15

Our words can glorify God with praise and thanksgiving or they can curse God with bitterness and ingratitude. Praise should always be the fruit of our lips. As there is no end to the greatness and goodness of God, so should there be no end to our praise!

How Great Thou Art

O Lord my God! When I in awesome wonder
Consider all the works Thy hand hath made.
I see the stars, I hear the rolling thunder,
Thy power throughout the universe displayed.

When through the woods and forest glades I wander
And hear the birds sing sweetly in the trees;
When I look down from lofty mountain grandeur
And hear the brook and feel the gentle breeze:

And when I think that God, His Son not sparing,
Sent Him to die, I scarce can take it in;
That on the cross, my burden gladly bearing,
He bled and died to take away my sin:

When Christ shall come with shout of acclamation
And take me home, what joy shall fill my heart!
Then I shall bow in humble adoration,
And there proclaim, my God, how great Thou art!

Refrain:
Then sings my soul, my Saviour God, to Thee:
How great Thou art, how great Thou art!
Then sings my soul, my Saviour God, to Thee:
How great Thou art, how great Thou art!

And it shall be said in that day,
Lo, this is our God; we have waited for him, and
he will save us;
this is the LORD; we have waited for him, we will be glad and
rejoice in his salvation. - Isaiah 25:9

The Waiting Period

GOD'S PROMISES MAY INCLUDE WAITING

Even with all confidence, illustrations, examples, promises, plans, and programs sometimes we are caught in confusion concerning how God answers prayer.

There are those times when God answers prayer almost immediately. Sometimes God answers our prayers virtually before we have prayed them. God knows our needs before we know them.

God answers immediately as we read in 12 Kings chapter 20 - *In those days was Hezekiah sick unto death. And the prophet Isaiah the son of Amoz came to him, and said unto him, Thus saith the LORD, Set thine house in order; for thou shalt die, and not live. Then he turned his face to the wall, and prayed unto the LORD, saying, I beseech thee, O LORD, remember now how I have walked before thee in truth and with a perfect heart, and have done that which is good in thy sight. And Hezekiah wept sore. And it came to pass, afore Isaiah was gone out into the middle court, that the word of the LORD came to him, saying, Turn again, and tell Hezekiah the captain of my people, Thus saith the LORD, the God of David thy father, I have heard thy prayer, I have seen thy tears: behold, I will heal thee: on the third day thou shalt go up unto the house of the LORD.* - 2 Kings 20:1-5

"Yes" is often the answer to our requests. Sometimes the answer is delayed. Sometimes the answer is in part and sometimes in whole. Sometimes we pray with perfect peace and assurance. Sometimes we pray seeking His guidance.

Sometimes He gives us our request when we would have been happier with "no!" *And he gave them their request; but sent leanness into their soul.* - Psalm 106:15

Sometimes God's answers are not what we imagined. Elijah prayed for God to kill Jezebel, but instead God took Elijah in a whirlwind - 2 Kings 2:11. Paul sought the Lord three times to be healed and God's answer was to give him the grace he needed to bear his infirmity. *For this thing I besought the Lord thrice, that it might depart from me. And he said unto me, My grace is sufficient for thee: for my strength is made perfect in weakness. Most gladly therefore will I rather glory in my infirmities, that the power of Christ may rest upon me.* - 2 Corinthians 12:8-9

Human beings hate to wait, and yet that is exactly what God requires of us. God often answers, "Wait". When God answers "Wait," it does not mean that God did not hear or that God does not care. God has a purpose in our waiting. There are many benefits in learning to wait. The Jeremiah said, *The LORD is good unto them that wait for him, to the soul that seeketh him. It is good that a man should both hope and quietly wait for the salvation of the LORD.* - Lamentations 3:25-26

God is never early and God is never late, but always right on time! God is never early and God is never late, but always right on time! We often learn life's most valuable lessons in the school of waiting. We must rest in the Lord lest we wrestle with the Lord.

There are many examples in the Bible of those who waited for an answer: Daniel waiting while the angels fought to deliver the answer, and the disciples praying through the night waiting for Peter to be delivered. Jesus taught in the model prayer, *"thy Kingdom come"*, and it is still coming! Believers Pray, *"Even so, come quickly Lord Jesus,"* and He is! We are to pray and wait!

Watch and Pray,
Stand Ready,
Listen for the Shout,
Seek the Lord for He is at Hand!

If you do not receive an answer and your faith begins to waiver, don't rest on your performance, trust His promises! Remember *"not my will, but thine be done."*

Do Not Give Up When God's Will Includes Waiting

It is easy to give up on God when God's will includes waiting. Abraham had faith to leave his home and sojourn in a foreign land, but he began to doubt when the wait for God's promise of a son took over 25 years to fulfill.

Now the LORD had said unto Abram, Get thee out of thy country, and from thy kindred, and from thy father's house, unto a land that I will shew thee: And I will make of thee a great nation, and I will bless thee, and make thy name great; and thou shalt be a blessing: - Genesis 12:1-2. Abram was 75 years old at the time of this promise. Genesis 12:4. Ten years later, Sarah and Abraham began to think that God needed help in fulfilling His promise and Ishmael is the result.

For the next 14 years, Abraham assumes that Ishmael is the promised heir. And then …25 years after His original promise, God appears to Abraham.

And God said unto Abraham, As for Sarai thy wife, thou shalt not call her name Sarai, but Sarah shall her name be. And I will bless her, and give thee a son also of her: yea, I will bless her, and she shall be a mother of nations; kings of people shall be of her. Then Abraham fell upon his face, and laughed, and said in his heart, Shall a child be born unto him that is an hundred years old? and shall Sarah, that is ninety years old, bear?… And God said, Sarah thy wife shall bear thee a son indeed; and thou shalt call his name Isaac: and I will establish my covenant with him for an everlasting covenant, and with his seed after him. - Genesis 17:15-17, 19

When the wait grows long, we are often tempted to 'help' God. Our human reasoning enters into the picture and we hatch our own plan, rather than waiting on God. We lack patience. But, the Bible encourages us to wait.

For ye have need of patience, that, after ye have done the will of God, ye might receive the promise. - Hebrews 10:36

Even though Abraham and Sarah had times when they doubted the promise of God, God kept His promise to Abraham. *And the LORD visited Sarah as he had said, and the LORD did unto Sarah as he had spoken. For Sarah conceived, and bare Abraham a son in his old age, at the set time of which God had spoken to him. ... And Abraham was an hundred years old, when his son Isaac was born unto him.* - Genesis 21:1-2, 5

Today, like Abraham and Sarah, we are waiting for a promise to be fulfilled. We are waiting for the promise of His return. It has been over 2000 years and we are still waiting like the children of Israel for His promise to be fulfilled.

God has given us a glimpse of the fulfilled promise in the Person of the Holy Spirit living within us, but there are those doubters who ridicule and challenge our belief. *Knowing this first, that there shall come in the last days scoffers, walking after their own lusts, And saying, Where is the promise of his coming? for since the fathers fell asleep, all things continue as they were from the beginning of the creation.* - 2 Peter 3:3-4

The Lord Jesus Christ knew our weakness in regard to waiting. His question should challenge our hearts to patiently wait and not give in to doubt and discouragement. *Nevertheless when the Son of man cometh, shall he find faith on the earth?* - Luke 18:8

Waiting in Hope Requires Patient Faith

But if we hope for that we see not, then do we with patience wait for it. - Romans 8:25 If we are weak in faith, God has made provision for our faith to increase. *So then faith cometh by hearing, and hearing by the word of God.* - Romans 10:17 There is abundant evidence that His promises contained in His Word are true. Even so, we don't always believe God and His Word to us. The result is that we live with many unmet needs that we attempt to satisfy through our own schemes and plots. God does not cast us off when our faith fails. *If we believe not, yet he abideth faithful: he cannot deny himself.* - 2 Timothy 2:13

Waiting requires us to trust in what we cannot see. It is important during long periods of waiting to keep our hearts and minds focused on God and on His promises. The longer we wait the more we are tempted to doubt God and His Word. We may be tempted to rely on our own reasoning and reject God's promises. We must choose to trust. *Trust in the LORD with all thine heart; and lean not unto thine own understanding.* - Proverbs 3:5

It is not always easy to wait and trust when we are hurting. There are times when we are burdened by the pressures we endure. There are times when we do not feel we can bear our situation another day or hour. The Psalmist

It is not always easy to wait and trust when we are hurting. There are times when we are burdened by the pressures we endure.

cried, *I am weary of my crying: my throat is dried: mine eyes fail while I wait for my God.* - Psalm 69:3 These are the times when our faith is truly tested. If we will wait and continue to trust Him, we will see His deliverance. He will become our source of strength and courage, not only for our present difficulties but for our future. *Wait on the LORD: be of good courage, and he shall strengthen thine heart: wait, I say, on the LORD.* - Psalm 27:14

God's promises are all true. God never fails to keep His promises. Sometimes, though, we have to wait years to see His promises fulfilled. We see the immediate. He sees the eternal. We are bound by time. He is everlasting. With Him a day is as a thousand years. 2 Peter 3:8. God sees the big picture. He sees the beginning and the ending at the same time. We only know and experience this one immediate point in time. God knows what we need now and in the future.

God has many reasons for having us wait. Learning to wait is a basic life skill. Anyone who has ever trained children knows they are not naturally patient! Even infants show impatience when they cry and scream for their next feeding. Older children may throw tantrums or cry when they must wait for what they want. You may have seen this vividly demonstrated when out shopping. You may have heard a child crying, whining, cajoling, begging and even

Learning to wait is a basic life skill.

ordering a parent who said, "Not now" to a request. This must be how we appear to God when He has answered, "Wait."

Many parents' hearts are broken over rebellious and prodigal children. Valerie was one of those parents. Her son moved away without even saying good-bye. Valerie had no address or phone number for her son. She shed many tears and prayed many days, weeks, months, and even years for his stubborn heart to turn back to God and the family he left. She frequently prayed that God would bring the right influences into his life.

Valerie did not know what was happening in her son's heart and mind. She did not know if he was well, what he was eating, where he was sleeping or if he was even safe. Valerie fasted and prayed and turned her son over to God completely. She knew God loved him even more than she did, and God would take care of her son, doing what was best in his life.

Not long after trusting her son totally to God's care, the phone rang and Valerie heard the word she longed to hear, "Mom". Like the prodigal son, Valerie's son learned some hard lessons, but the most important lesson he learned was that his mother loved him, and God loved him even more. No one in the world cared for him like his mom or like His God.

Waiting builds and challenges our patience, and patience is a basic ingredient in the process of spiritual growth. Paul outlined it this way: *knowing that tribulation worketh patience; And patience, experience; and experience, hope: And hope maketh not ashamed; because the love of God is shed abroad in our hearts by the Holy Ghost which is given unto us.* - Romans 5:3-5

WAITING BUILDS FAITH

We can see from the Bible that faith building is a cycle. First, God reveals a promise to us. Then we choose to trust God to fulfill His promise and then we wait. Finally, He graciously fulfills His promise! The result should be our praising Him and the strengthening of our faith to patiently wait again. *I will praise thee for ever, because thou hast done it: and I will wait on thy name; for it is good before thy saints.* - Psalm 52:9

Those who have trusted God and His promises in the face of great adversity have seen His deliverance as a result. They have a confidence and a courage that others do not. David may not have had the boldness to face Goliath had he not already seen God deliver him from the bear and the lion. (1 Samuel 17:34-36) When we trust and wait we learn to face life with an unusual boldness and certainty. When we see His deliverance in one area of life, we are more willing to step out by faith and trust God, regardless of what the future may hold.

What should we do while waiting? The mistake we may be tempted to make is that of putting life on hold. Life goes on while we wait. We have duties and responsibilities, as well as joys and pleasures that should not be ignored while we wait. The psalmist put it this way, *Trust in the LORD, and do good; so shalt thou dwell in the land, and verily thou shalt be fed.* - Psalm 37:3

There are three things to note in this verse. In the first part of the verse we read, *"Trust in the Lord, and do good;"* We are to do good. We are to accomplish our duties while we wait. A well-known psychologist asked his women clients, "Is your ironing done?" (This was back in the day before permanent press!) When they answered, "No, it is piled up." He knew they were most likely dealing with depression. There are several causes for depression. We may find that the strain of waiting brings with it disappointment and discouragement and these can easily lead to depression. God, of course, understands our weaknesses and provides these words of wisdom: trust and do good. We may think that focusing on what we need and want will bring it about sooner but changing our focus to what we need to accomplish today brings balance to our lives.

The second part of Psalm 37:3 reads, *"so shalt thou dwell in the land."* If we will focus on our daily lives and responsibilities, we will enjoy many victories. There are daily obstacles to overcome in the strength of Our God. They may be as simple as balancing a checkbook, learning a new skill, or teaching a child to tie their shoes, or they may be as difficult as communicating with our spouse or teaching our teenager to drive. As we trust God and succeed at the daily challenges of life, we not only gain confidence in God's ability and willingness to meet our needs and answer our prayers, we also experience personal satisfaction over our accomplishments.

Finally, the verse concludes, *"and verily thou shalt be fed."* We can allow ourselves to be so consumed with our waiting that we miss out on the joys and pleasures God has for us today. Jesus taught us to pray, *Give us this day our daily bread.* - Matthew 6:11

And the psalmist said, *Blessed be the Lord, who daily loadeth us with benefits, even the God of our salvation. Selah.* - Psalm 68:19 If we will but look for them, we will see that every day God gives us a myriad of blessings. When we ignore those blessings, we become unthankful and ungrateful.

Yes, waiting can be difficult, and our need can be crucial, but our faith is not strengthened by focusing on our need but rather upon the supplier of all of our wants and needs. When we look for and focus on all of the wonderful things and many blessings God provides for us on a daily basis, our hearts find reason to rejoice in the midst of our trials. As we trust in the God who feeds the sparrows, and our prayers grow in confidence and frequency. In this place we discover *the peace that passeth all understanding.*

Be careful for nothing; but in every thing by prayer and supplication with thanksgiving let your requests be made known unto God. And the peace of God, which passeth all understanding, shall keep your hearts and minds through Christ Jesus. - Philippians 4:6-7

FAITH MUST BE BASED ON HIS PROMISES

Ignorance of God's Word robs us of the promises given in those precious pages. Jesus told the Pharisees, *Search the scriptures; for in them ye think ye have eternal life: and they are they which testify of me.* - John 5:39

Promises are woven throughout God's Word. They are there for our benefit, for our learning. Our faith must be based upon the Word of God.

God not only provides food for our physical bodies, but also for our spirits. We cannot summon up the faith we need to wait on the Lord. There is only one source for such faith. *So then faith cometh by hearing, and hearing by the word of God.* - Romans 10:17. Faith defeats discouragement. Faith is the weapon God gives us to overcome all of our desperation and anxiety. *For whatsoever is born of God overcometh the world: and this is the victory that overcometh the world, even our faith.* - 1 John 5:4 As you have read through this book, you may have noted the many scripture passages we have quoted. Our opinions are of little value. It is God's Word that reveals to us the truth and brings with it the faith we need to believe, trust, and wait.

God has provided and purchased all we need.

JOURNALING TIPS

Praise and thanksgiving are the antidote for fear and doubt. When it seems that our wait is longer than we can bear and when we begin to doubt God's promises it is time to defeat that fear and doubt with words of praise and thanksgiving.

It helps if you plan how you will praise and thank God. Writing down our praises helps us to remember all God's blessings. We find three areas of praise and thanksgiving in our Bible: Names of God, Attributes of God, Actions of God.

As you read through your Bible begin listing all of the names of God.

King of Kings	*Lord of Lords*	*Creator*
The Way	*Truth*	*Life*
Creator	*Counselor*	*Redeemer*

Also, begin listing the many adjectives used to describe God.

Wonderful	*Mighty*	*Great*
Glorious	*Merciful*	*Holy*

Finally, praise and thank God for the things He has done.
Thank you Lord for your magnificent creation!
Thank you Lord for providing all my needs.
Thank you Lord for loving me and sending Jesus.
Thank you Lord for your protection.
Thank you Lord for your guidance.

That Christ may dwell in your hearts by faith; that ye, being rooted and grounded in love, May be able to comprehend with all saints what is the breadth, and length, and depth, and height; And to know the love of Christ, which passeth knowledge, that ye might be filled with *all the fulness of God.*

- Ephesians 3:17-19

Conclusion

WE MUST NOT FEAR CHANGE

Why do people choose to live so far below their inheritance in Christ? Why do they stay in dehumanizing relationships? Why do they suffer unnecessarily? Psychologists could give us a lengthy list of reasons for self-destructive behaviors and beliefs. Certainly, fear of change must be one of the most common. Entire books have been written on the fear of change. Very few people embrace change. The familiar is comfortable and predictable. Change brings with it the unknown and unpredictable.

Receiving the promises of God guarantees change. The very nature of the Christian life is change. All of it is good change, but it is change none-the-less. Change from death to life. Change from guilt to forgiveness. Change from poverty to abundance. Change from rejection to acceptance.

God promises change. *to give unto them beauty for ashes, the oil of joy for mourning, the garment of praise for the spirit of heaviness; that they might be called trees of righteousness, the planting of the LORD, that he might be glorified.* - Isaiah 61:3

To enjoy the fulfilled promises of God we must boldly and courageously embrace change.

WE MUST ABANDON SELF-PITY

Children learn what works. In some homes it works to pout and sulk. Parents may give in to a poochy lip and sullen demeanor. They may go to great lengths to cheer up their despondent offspring. Because it works, this same strategy may be carried into adulthood. It may be tried on friends, spouses, fellow employees and church members.

Self-pity has its rewards. The belief that life is not fair, and I am its victim allows us to justify many selfish behaviors. We tell ourselves we are not responsible for outcomes. It relieves us of responsibility and demands sympathy from others. Answered prayer removes any justification for self-pity.

WE MUST TAKE THESE STEPS

No matter what your history, no matter what trials you are facing now, no matter who you are or where you are, God always keeps His promises. To realize the fulfillment of God's promises in your life we recommend these steps.

Begin by asking. Ask God specifically for what you need in your life right now. Come to Him seeking and expecting Him to answer you as a father answers his beloved child. Claim the promises God gives to you. You must ask to receive. The prodigal son believed that his father would receive him and cloth and feed him, but he had to return to the father. Only in the presence of his father would his needs be met. Only in relationship with our Heavenly Father are our needs met. God is waiting for us to draw nigh to Him and ask with childlike faith.[46]

---

46   *Draw nigh to God, and he will draw nigh to you. Cleanse your hands, ye sinners; and purify your hearts, ye double minded.* - James 4:8

Put God and His will for your life first. Do not hesitate to ask God for the desires of your heart, delighting in Him and in His purpose. What you need is not always what you think you want. What you ask for is not always what you need or even what has been given to you. The most important qualifier of any promise is God's will not ours. Most people pray their will be done, not God's will.

Pray through the Bible. Pray according to the Word of God. Base your prayers on the Word of God and not your feelings. Use your journal to record the promises you are claiming while listing the corresponding conditions.

Apart from His promise of eternal life,[47] His greatest promise to us is His promise to come again.[48] Are you waiting? Is your heart comforted in knowing that He has prepared a place for you? That He has not forgotten? Is your hope in Him? All of our answered prayers and all of His fulfilled promises to us in this life are merely a preamble to the fulfillment of His greatest promises to us.

And the Lord direct your hearts into the love of God, and into the patient waiting for Christ. - 2 Thessalonians 3:5

Waiting requires us to trust in what we cannot see. It is important during long periods of waiting to keep our hearts and minds focused on God and on His promises.[49]
How do you wait? In a doctor's waiting room there are different kinds of waiting. Some people are frustrated and anxious because they must wait. Some talk on their phones or traipse back and forth from the front desk, loudly complaining to whoever will listen that they are waiting. Others just slump in a chair depressed by the wait. And then others come prepared to wait. They bring things to do while they wait. They keep busy while they wait. All of these people know that they will eventually see the

---

47   *And this is the record, that God hath given to us eternal life, and this life is in his Son. He that hath the Son hath life; and he that hath not the Son of God hath not life. - 1 John 5:11-12.*

48   *And if I go and prepare a place for you, I will come again, and receive you unto myself; that where I am, there ye may be also. - John 14:3.*

49   *This I recall to my mind, therefore have I hope. It is of the LORD'S mercies that we are not consumed, because his compassions fail not. They are new every morning: great is thy faithfulness. The LORD is my portion, saith my soul; therefore will I hope in him. The LORD is good unto them that wait for him, to the soul that seeketh him. It is good that a man should both hope and quietly wait for the salvation of the LORD. - Lamentations 3:21-26*

69

doctor. We know the Lord is going to answer our prayers. In the meantime, we need to keep busy while we wait.

We must fill our thoughts, our hearts, and our mouths with praise for our God![50] Speak the things that are true. Satan is a liar and we repeat his lies. Truth is based upon the Word of God. It is not extrapolated from the Word of God. We must seek the whole counsel of God as we claim the promises He has clearly given us in His Word.

We can build a life of praise by meditating on His Word, remembering His wonderful works to the children of men.[51]

Do we waver in our belief that God's miraculous power is available to us simply for the asking? Do we hesitate to trust Him for great things?

Writing down our answers to prayer and the many promises God fulfills for us is a good way to recall all He has done for us. Remembering builds our faith and gives us confidence in the future.

Everyday should be another opportunity for God to do great things in our life. We should wake every morning with great expectations for a miraculous walk with God.

JOURNALING TIPS

Start Today!

If you have not already done so, start today recording God's promises and His answers to your prayers. The more we pray and the more we practice believing God, the more opportunity we have to see His mighty works in our own lives.

---

50   *I will bless the LORD at all times: his praise shall continually be in my mouth. - Psalm 34:1*
51   *Oh that men would praise the LORD for his goodness, and for his wonderful works to the children of men! - Psalm 107:8*

Made in the
USA
Columbia, SC